Willowisp SUPERBOOKS

The Superbook of OUR UNIVERSE

James Muirden

D1298105

Willowisp Press

Contents

First published in this edition by Willowisp Press, Inc. 1987.
© Grisewood & Dempsey Limited 1981, 1986.
Printed in Hong Kong.

ISBN 0-87406-225-X

Cover Design by the Pinpoint Design Company

The Universe

To someone standing on the earth's surface two thousand years ago, the sun, the moon, and the objects in the night sky would have looked much the same as they do today. But the earth itself was not the same. To an observer out in space, earth would have shown few signs of life. Only a powerful telescope could have detected the scattered cities and settlements, and the night hemisphere would have been black and dead. Now, however, someone standing on the moon, just using binoculars, could make out places like New York and London. When night falls, lights glow in the darkness. Satellites circle the globe, and every now and then a spaceship soars out into space.

Today, although the sky looks no different, we have learned to look at it in a different way. The invention of the telescope has brought the stars and planets closer and taught us many new facts. Now space vehicles are opening up a new age of discovery. The first twenty years of the Space Age have taught us more about the Solar System than we had ever been able to find out before.

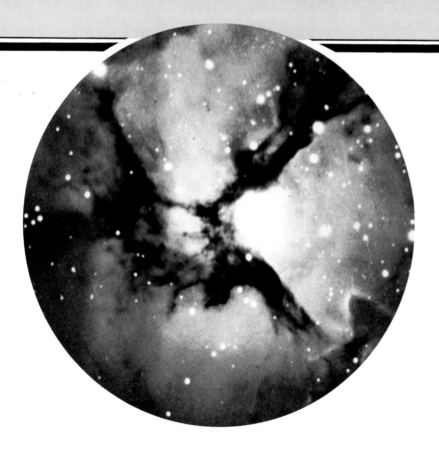

We live on a whirling platform in space – our planet earth. Eight other planets, four larger and four smaller, whirl with us. All are held in their orbits around the sun, our star, by the pull of gravity.

Our solar system is about 4,600 million years old. The universe is probably four times older than this. The galaxy called the Milky Way, in which the sun lies, is almost as old as the universe, but stars inside it are dying of old age, while others are being born. The sun is a youngster compared with some of the stars seen in the sky.

The planets in the solar system are as old as the sun. They all formed inside a huge cloud of dark gas and dust. The sun grew big and hot and started to shine. The planets, so much smaller, never grew hot enough to shine, except by the reflected light of the sun.

▲ Astronomers believe that time and the universe began about 20 billion years ago. All the material that now forms living things, planets and stars, exploded in the Big Bang and later condensed into galaxies.

System

▶ Each planet rotates on its axis as it orbits the sun. Uranus and Pluto (not shown) are tilted on their side. This drawing is not to scale.

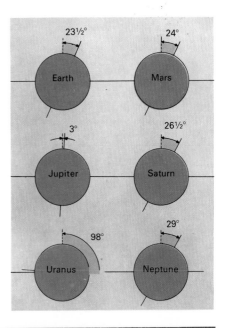

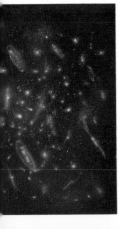

▼ The nine major planets of the solar system, in order outward from the sun, are shown here. The four closest planets to the sun (Mercury, Venus, Earth, and Mars) are small with rocky surfaces, and are known as the terrestrial planets. Next come the four giant planets (Jupiter, Saturn, Uranus, and Neptune), which are made up of frozen, soupy gases. Apart from Neptune, which is hard to observe, they all have large families of satellites, as well as bright or faint rings of countless tiny orbiting bodies. Tiny Pluto has a single satellite. The sizes of the planets are to scale, but they are shown much too close together.

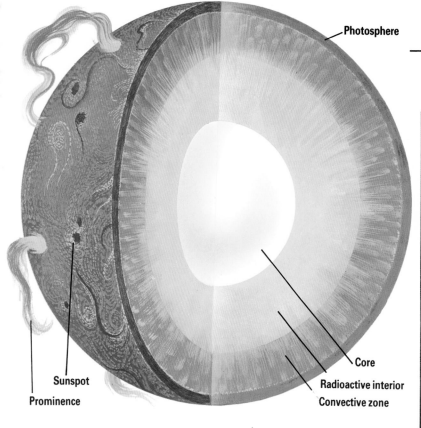

Photosphere

Sunspot

Prominence

Core

Radioactive interior

Convective zone

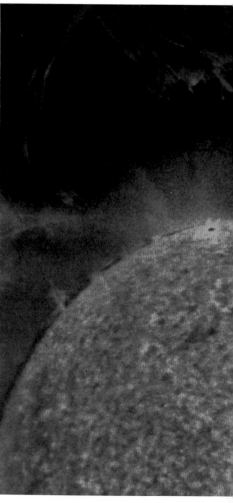

▲ The sun's energy source is hidden near its center, but this is how it might look if we could see inside. Nine-tenths of the sun consists of hydrogen, which is the commonest element in the universe, and inside the hot core this hydrogen is being changed into helium. The energy from this reaction heats the upper layers of the star and bursts into space from the turbulent surface.

▶ The sun's surface or photospere boils and seethes at a temperature of 6,000°C – far above that of any furnace. Jets of shining hydrogen known as prominences are shot into space at speeds of hundreds of miles per second.

Eclipses

▲ All planets and satellites cast their own shadow in space, where the sun's light is cut off. Around this dark shadow, or umbra, there is a lighter region, the penumbra, where the sunlight is only partly dimmed. When

the moon is exactly between the earth and the sun, and its shadow falls on the earth's surface, an eclipse of the sun is seen. To see a total eclipse, the observer must be standing in the umbra.

▲ At a total eclipse of the sun, the dazzling photospere is hidden by the moon, and the faint outer atmosphere or corona comes into view. A total eclipse can never last longer than 7½ minutes.

Sun

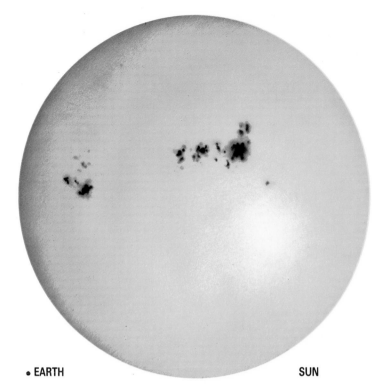

• EARTH   SUN

▲ Sunspots are cool areas on the sun's surface, and they are most common every 11 years or so (as in 1969 and 1980). To estimate the size of a sunspot group, remember that the sun is 100 times the diameter of the earth. A huge group such as the one shown here may survive for months, but most spots last for less than a fortnight.

▼ A prominence bursts upward from the edge of the sun. It is a tongue of hydrogen at 50,000°C or more, and could swallow and shrivel the earth. The eruption shown in these photographs lasted for only six minutes.

FACTS ABOUT THE SUN

Diameter: 865,318 miles (1,392,530 km).

Density: 1·41 times water.

Mass: 333,000 times the earth.

Surface temperature: 6,000°C.

Rotation period: 25 days 9 hours.

Age: about 4·6 billion years.

Cycle of sunspot activity: about 11 years.

Distance of nearest star: 4·3 light-years.

Distance to the center of the Galaxy: 30,000 light-years.

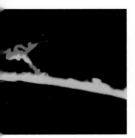
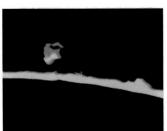

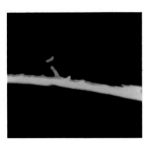

—Scorched

Mercury is never more than 28° away from the sun (slightly more than the angle from tip of thumb to little finger at arm's length). The only time it can be seen with the naked eye is when it shines low in the sky over the sunrise or sunset point.

Before the U.S. Mariner 10 probe visited Mercury in 1974, astronomers had seen only faint smudges on the planet's disk, and the best views showed less detail than the moon shows to the naked eye.

Crust

Mantle

Core

▲ Mercury, the second-smallest planet in the solar system, is not much larger than the moon, and its surface is covered with lunar-type craters. Its huge iron core makes it denser than any planet apart from the earth. All four terrestrial planets contain a great deal of iron, silicon, and other heavy elements.

► If people ever venture to Mercury, they will walk over the bleached bones of a dead world. It is airless and dry, and the daytime surface roasts beneath the searing sun, while by night it is much colder than anywhere on the earth.

Mercury whirls around the sun in only 88 days, the length of its year, but it takes 59 days to rotate once on its axis. This means that the sun moves very slowly across the sky, taking over three months to pass from one horizon to the other. When it was a young planet, Mercury probably spun on its axis in just a few hours. The gravitational pull of the sun has slowed it down, just as the earth's pull has braked the moon's spin and forced one hemisphere to remain turned toward us.

It seems impossible that any life forms known to us could survive on Mercury. If they were not killed by the heat, they would have to withstand deadly radiation from the sun that destroys living cells.

Mercury

JOURNEY

But Mariner 10 passed only a few hundred miles away from the planet's surface, and sent back amazingly detailed pictures.

Mercury's surface, like the moon's, was bombarded with rocky interplanetary bodies soon after it was formed. These made huge splashes that we now see as craters. There are also valleys and mountain chains, formed long ago when the planet's crust stretched and wrinkled like a thin skin.

▲ The surface of Mercury photographed from Mariner.

▶ The diameter of Mercury is less than the distance across Africa.

Earth   Mercury

FACTS ABOUT MERCURY

Diameter: 3,031 miles (4,878 km).
Density: 5·43 times water.
Mass: 0·055 of the earth.
Surface temperature: 660°F (noon), −330°F (night).
Length of year: 88 days.
Rotation period: 58·6 days.
Mean distance from sun: 35,979,000 miles (57,900,000 km).
Mean velocity in orbit: 29·7 miles (47·9 km) per second.
Tilt of axis: about 25°.
Escape velocity: 2·6 miles (4·2 km) per second.
Force of gravity at surface: 0·37 of the earth.
Atmosphere: none.
Known satellites: none.

▶ In Greek mythology Mercury, being the fastest-moving planet, ran errands for the other gods. This is the symbol for Mercury.

9

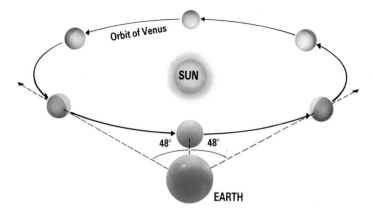

Orbit of Venus

SUN

48° 48°

EARTH

▲ Venus, like Mercury, seems to swing around the sun, but it is much easier to see. When it is near elongation (the position marked by the dotted lines) it is bright enough to be seen with the naked eye in full daylight, if its position in the sky is accurately known. Venus shines so brightly because of its thick atmosphere, which reflects sunlight much better than does a bare, rocky surface.

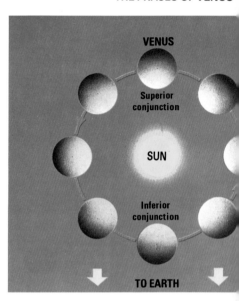

THE PHASES OF VENUS

VENUS

Superior conjunction

SUN

Inferior conjunction

TO EARTH

Inferior conjunction

▲ This photograph, taken by the interplanetary probe Mariner 10 in 1974, shows the all-covering cloudy atmosphere of Venus. It is much thicker than the earth's atmosphere, and consists of unbreathable carbon dioxide and sulfuric acid vapor. Because of the way the atmosphere blankets in the heat (known as the "greenhouse effect"), the surface of Venus is much hotter than the day side of Mercury.

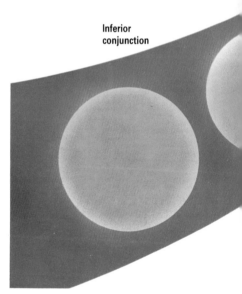

▲ Venus shows phases like the moon. At superior conjunction, the sunlit hemisphere is turned directly toward the earth. At inferior conjunction, we can see only the dark side (although a thin crescent is usually visible). Venus also appears much larger at inferior conjunction, because it is then that it is at its closest to the earth.

Venus

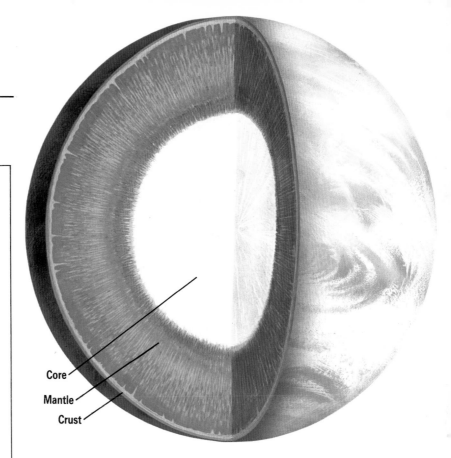

Core

Mantle

Crust

▲ Venus and the earth are almost identical twins in size and makeup, with large cores of iron, nickel, and other metals. The surfaces of the two planets are completely different because plant growth never occurred on Venus. If it had, the plants would have turned the carbon dioxide into oxygen, and higher life might have flourished.

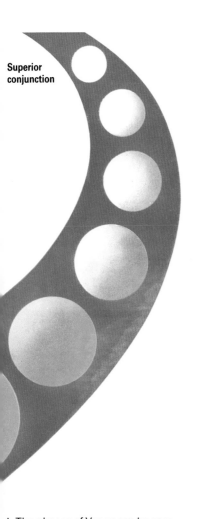

Superior conjunction

▲ The phases of Venus can be seen with a pair of binoculars, and the famous astronomer, Galileo, observed them in 1610 with his primitive telescope. At that time, most people believed that the sun and the planets all moved around the earth, and that Venus was always closer than the sun. Galileo showed that Venus must be moving around the sun, and this was one of the first proofs that the earth-centered theory was wrong.

Venus rotates on its axis in 243 days, which is longer than its year of 225 days. The sun (if it could be seen through the clouds) would rise in the west and set in the east over 3½ earth years later.

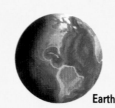

Earth   Venus

FACTS ABOUT VENUS

Diameter: 7,521 miles (12,104 km).
Density: 5·24 times water.
Mass: 0·82 of the earth.
Surface temperature: about 930°F (day side).
Length of year: 225 days.
Rotation period: 243 days.
Mean distance from sun: 67,235,480 miles (108,200,000 km).
Mean velocity in orbit: 21·7 miles (35·0 km) per second.
Tilt of axis: 3°.
Escape velocity: 6·4 miles (10·3 km) per second.
Force of gravity at surface: 0·88 of the earth.
Atmosphere: about 90 times the density of the earth's; main constituent, carbon dioxide.
Known satellites: none.

Earth's Atmosphere

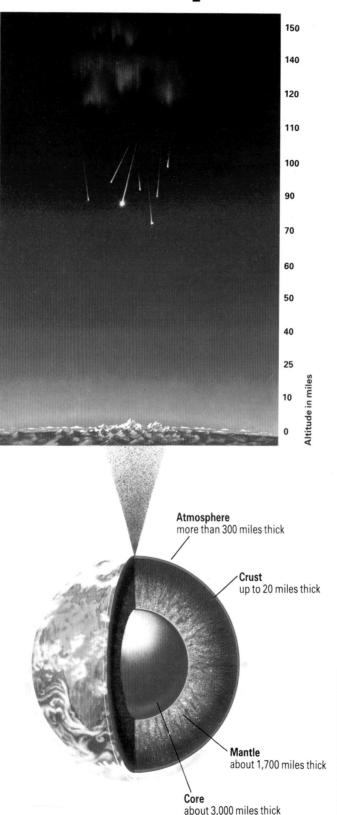

Atmosphere
more than 300 miles thick

Crust
up to 20 miles thick

Mantle
about 1,700 miles thick

Core
about 3,000 miles thick

◄ The Earth's atmosphere contains 21% oxygen. Most of the rest is nitrogen. The atmosphere contains so much oxygen because plants release it as they grow. If plant life disappeared, so would the oxygen, and animal life would die.

The upper regions of the atmosphere are very thin. Even at a height of 6 miles (10 kilometers), it is only one third as dense as at sea level. The very thin ozone layer 15 miles (25 kilometers) up is vitally important, because it absorbs dangerous radiations from the sun. Meteors (flying interplanetary particles) are burned up at heights of about 62 miles (100 kilometers), while auroras occur at still greater altitudes.

▲ Auroras are caused by particles emitted by the sun, which make the upper atmosphere glow. They usually occur over the earth's poles. Ordinary auroras are no more than a dim glow near the horizon, but bright arches are sometimes seen.

Earth

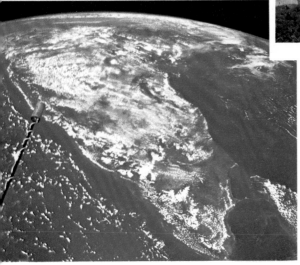

◀ The earth teems with a fantastic variety of life, whereas the other planets of the solar system appear to be lifeless. If our world was only a few million miles closer to the sun, it might be a choking inferno like Venus. If it was a little farther away, it would be a bitterly cold waste like the planet Mars.

▲ A photograph such as this one, taken from a satellite, reveals the earth as just another planet. But it is unique in the solar system in having huge wastes of water on its surface.

▼ The earth spins around its axis once a day. This axis always points in the same direction in space as the earth follows its yearly course around the sun. The north pole is tilted as its greatest angle towards the sun on June 21, bringing summer to the northern hemisphere. At mid-winter (December 21), the north pole is turned away from the sun, which appears low in the sky, and the days are at their shortest.

FACTS ABOUT THE EARTH

Diameter: 7,926 miles (12,756 km), equatorial, 7,900 miles (12,714 km) polar.
Density: 5·52 times water.
Mean temperature: 72°F.
Length of year: 365¼ days.
Rotation period: 23 hours 56 minutes.
Mean distance from the sun: 92,960,000 miles (149,600,000 km).
Mean velocity in orbit: 18·5 miles (29·8 km) per second.
Tilt of axis: 23½°.
Escape velocity: 6·96 miles (11·2 km) per second.
Atmosphere: main constituents are nitrogen (78½%) and oxygen (21%).
Crust: main constituents are oxygen (47%), silicon (28%), aluminum (8%), and iron (5%).
Area of land surface: 57,268,965 sq. miles (148,326,000 sq. km), 29% of total surface.
Area of water surface: 139,668,537 sq. miles (361,740,000 sq. km), 71% of total surface.
Highest mountain peak: Mount Everest, 29,000 feet (8,848 meters) above sea level.
Greatest depression: Mariana Trench, Pacific Ocean, drops to 36,000 feet (11,033 meters) below sea level.
Oldest known rocks: Archaean rocks (Canada); age 3·7 billion years.
Known satellites: one.

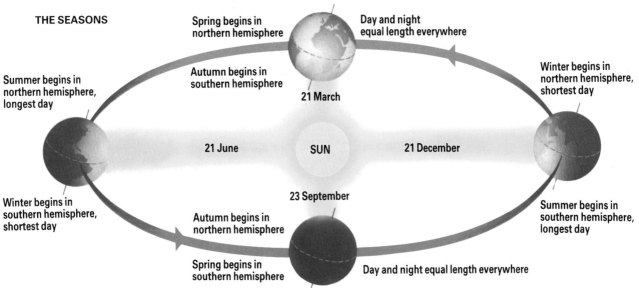

THE SEASONS

Spring begins in northern hemisphere

Autumn begins in southern hemisphere

21 March

Day and night equal length everywhere

Winter begins in northern hemisphere, shortest day

Summer begins in northern hemisphere, longest day

21 June

SUN

21 December

Winter begins in southern hemisphere, shortest day

Autumn begins in northern hemisphere

23 September

Spring begins in southern hemisphere

Day and night equal length everywhere

Summer begins in southern hemisphere, longest day

FACTS ABOUT THE MOON

Diameter: 2,160 miles (3,476 km).
Density: 3·34 times water.
Mass: 0·012 of the earth.
Surface temperature: 210°F (noon), −240°F (night).
Lunar month (New Moon to New Moon): 29 days 13 hours.
Mean distance from earth: 238,866 miles (384,400 km).
Mean velocity in orbit: 0·62 miles (1·0 km) per second.
Tilt of axis: 1½°.
Escape velocity: 1·5 miles (2·4 km) per second.
Force of gravity at surface: 0·16 of the earth.
Atmosphere: none.

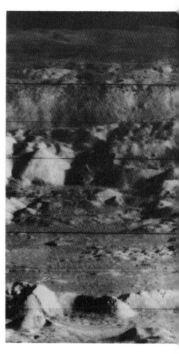

▶ The diameter of the moon is about the same as the distance across Australia. It is the sixth largest satellite in the solar system, but (apart from Pluto's moon) it is the largest compared with its parent planet.

▼ The moon passes through a complete cycle of phases in 29½ days. At New Moon, when the dark hemisphere is turned toward us, the moon is very near the sun in the sky and cannot be seen. If the line-up is perfect, it blocks out the sun in a solar eclipse, but this usually happens only a couple of times a year. Two or three days later, it becomes visible in the evening sky as a thin crescent. It grows larger night by night until it becomes a perfect half-moon in the First Quarter position. A week later it is Full, and then it wanes through the Last Quarter to another New Moon phase. This picture is not to scale.

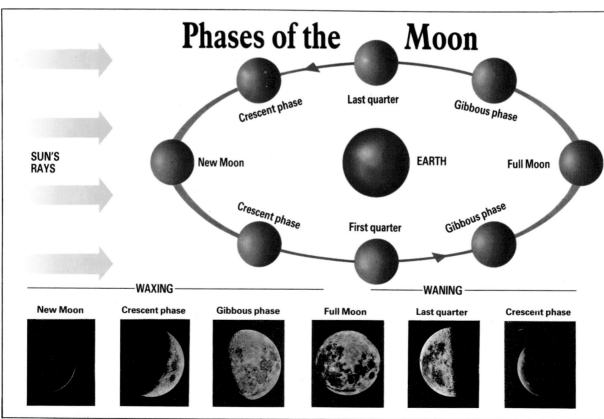

Phases of the Moon

SUN'S RAYS

Crescent phase · Last quarter · Gibbous phase

New Moon · EARTH · Full Moon

Crescent phase · First quarter · Gibbous phase

———— WAXING ———— ———— WANING ————

| New Moon | Crescent phase | Gibbous phase | Full Moon | Last quarter | Crescent phase |

Moon

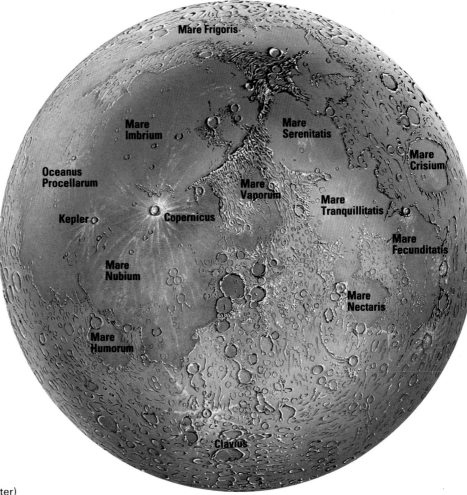

▲ A view of the 56-mile (90-kilometer) crater Copernicus, photographed by an Orbiter lunar satellite that mapped the surface for the Apollo landings. The foreground peaks are about 3,280 feet (1,000 meters).

▼ A solar eclipse occurs when the moon's shadow falls on the earth's surface. A lunar eclipse occurs when the moon passes through the earth's shadow at the Full Moon. (Not shown to scale.)

▲ This map shows the most important details on the moon's earth-turned hemisphere. There are large dark plains such as *Mare Serenitatis* (Sea of Serenity), huge mountain chains, and the craters formed when interplanetary bodies collided with the moon soon after it condensed into a globe. The "seas" are probably the youngest features. They formed when lava flowed out from beneath the crust and drowned the older craters altogether.

Rock samples that have been brought back to earth show that no important surface change has happened in the last 3 billion years or so – about the time it has taken life to evolve on earth. The moon's gravity is too weak to hold on to any atmosphere, and any water on its surface would quickly disappear into space. We are looking at a fossilized world.

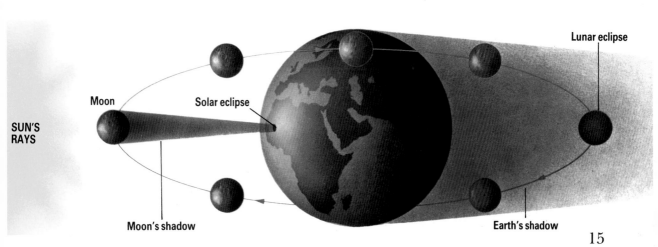

15

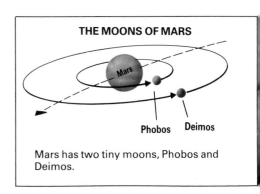

THE MOONS OF MARS

Mars has two tiny moons, Phobos and Deimos.

▲ Mars has always fascinated astronomers. Its atmosphere is thin enough to let the surface be seen, but thick enough to give some protection for simple life forms. Seen from the earth, it shows white polar caps and dark markings. Sometimes great dust storms hide these features. Spacecraft proved that the surface of Mars is a cross between those of the moon and the earth.

▶ This has been described as the picture of the century. It was taken by Viking I, which landed on Mars in 1976, and shows loose boulders and stones as small as half an inch across. The two Viking probes did not find any proof of life on Mars, but this does not mean that life does not exist. There are more sheltered places on the planet, unvisited by spacecraft, where simple organisms might survive.

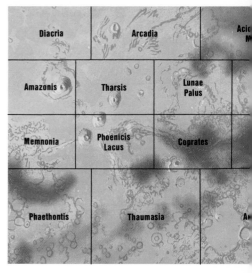

Diacria · Arcadia · Acic
Amazonis · Tharsis · Lunae Palus
Memnonia · Phoenicis Lacus · Coprates
Phaethontis · Thaumasia

▶ This map of mars was drawn from photographs taken by Mariner 9, which went into orbit around the planet in 1971. Ancient craters, like the ones on the moon, cover much of the surface, but there are also dusty deserts and, near the left edge, huge volcanic mountains up to 18 miles (30 kilometers) high.

Mars

▶ Although Mars is much smaller than the earth, it is like our planet in many ways. It has a large iron core, and lava from the interior can still force its way to the surface through weak points in the crust. But it has only a thin atmosphere, and no rainfall, and the surface temperature is always below freezing point. Even so, it is the most earthlike planet.

Core —————————————

Mantle —————————————

Crust —————————————

Ismenius Lacus	Casius	Cebrenia
Arabia	Syrtis Major	Amenthes
Sabaeus Sinus	iapigia	Tyrrhenum Mare
Noachis	Hellas	Eridania

▼ Mars is much smaller than the earth, but when nearest to us it shines with a brilliant reddish color. In Roman mythology, Mars was the god of war.

Earth   Mars

FACTS ABOUT MARS

Diameter: 4,221 miles (6,794 km).
Density: 3·93 times water.
Mass: 0·11 of earth.
Surface temperature in summer: −4°F (noon), −112°F (night).
Length of year: 687 days.
Rotation period: 24 hours 37 minutes.
Mean distance from the sun: 141,600,000 miles (227,900,000 km).
Mean velocity in orbit: 15 miles (24·1 km) per second.
Tilt of axis: 24°.
Escape velocity: 3·11 miles (5·0 km) per second.
Force of gravity at surface: 0·38 of the earth.
Atmosphere: about 1/100th the density of the earth's; main constituent, carbon dioxide.
Known satellites: two.

Jupiter

Earth

Jupiter

FACTS ABOUT JUPITER

Diameter: 88,736 miles (142,800 km)
equatorial 83,391 miles (134,200 km) polar.
Density: 1·32 times water.
Mass: 318 times the earth.
Temperature of cloud surface: −240°F.
Length of year: 11·9 years.
Rotation period: 9 hours 50 minutes.
Mean distance from the sun: 483,635,620 miles
(778,300,000 km).
Tilt of axis: 3°.
Atmosphere: main constituents hydrogen and
helium.
Known satellites: 16.

▲ In 1979 the two Voyager spacecraft took amazingly detailed
photographs of Jupiter and its satellites. Five separate pictures
have been combined here to give an imaginary view of Jupiter
with its four largest satellites in the foreground. Jupiter's great
red spot can be seen: a gigantic whirlpool about three times
the size of the earth. Voyager also discovered a very faint ring
around the planet.

▼ Like the sun and the other three giant planets, about
90% of Jupiter is made up of hydrogen, the lightest
element in the universe. Near the surface, the hydrogen
atoms have combined with atoms of oxygen to form
water (frozen into ice), and with atoms of nitrogen to form
ammonia. There are many other compounds too. Deeper
inside the planet, hydrogen gas is compressed into a
liquid. Jupiter spins on its axis in a shorter time than any
other planet, and the centrifugal force makes it bulge
outward at the equator.

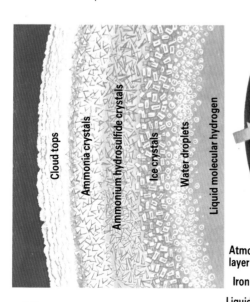

Cloud tops

Ammonia crystals

Ammonium hydrosulfide crystals

Ice crystals

Water droplets

Liquid molecular hydrogen

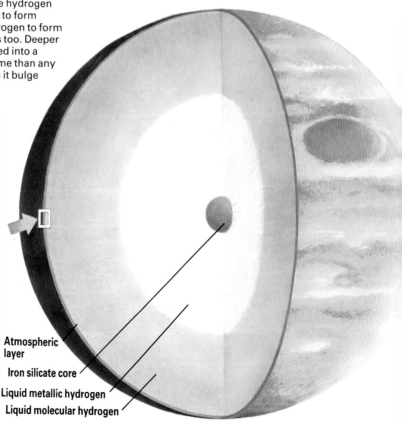

Atmospheric
layer

Iron silicate core

Liquid metallic hydrogen

Liquid molecular hydrogen

Saturn

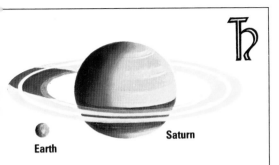

Earth   **Saturn**

FACTS ABOUT SATURN

Diameter: 74,568 miles (120,000 km) equatorial, 67,000 miles (108,000 km) polar.
Density: 0·70 of water.
Mass: 95 times the Earth.
Temperature of cloud surface: −290°F.
Length of year: 29·5 years.
Rotation period: 10 hours 14 minutes.
Mean distance from the Sun: 886,740,000 miles (1,427,000,000 km).
Tilt of axis: 27°.
Atmosphere: main constituents hydrogen, helium.
Known satellites: 21.

▲ Saturn is famous for its ring system. From the earth they appear smooth, but Voyager's photographs like this one show that they are braided into hundreds of separate strands. Although they are over twenty times the diameter of the earth, they are only a few miles thick. They consist of tiny particles of space debris. There are three main rings and many narrow faint ones. Saturn itself shows bright and dark markings, like Jupiter, but its surface is not nearly so turbulent. There are no permanent markings like the Great Red Spot.

1966   **1973**

1980   **1988**

◄ Saturn's axis is tilted, which means that, as it goes around the sun in the course of its long year, first one pole and then the other points inward toward the sun and the earth. The way in which we see the ring system changes as well. In 1980, the rings were edge-on and difficult to see for a few days. In 1988, they will be as wide open as they ever can be.

Ring C (the inner ring) has so few particles that the planet can be seen shining through it. Between outer ring A and middle ring B is a clear gap called Cassini's Division. The Voyager probes have discovered other very faint rings, which are difficult or impossible to see from the earth.

◄ Uranus is so remote and dim that little was known about it until Voyager 2 visited the planet in 1986. It spins on its side, so that at certain times one of its poles is turned toward the sun.

Uranus has 15 known satellites. The 5 biggest are shown in this photograph. The "steering wheel" effect is a photographic fault. Its ring system, discovered in 1977, is very faint.

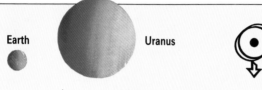

Earth   Uranus

FACTS ABOUT URANUS

Diameter: about 32,310 miles (52,000 km).
Density: 1·25 times water.
Mass: 14·6 times the earth.
Temperature of cloud surface: −6°F.
Length of year: 84·0 years.
Rotation period: 16 hours 50 minutes.
Mean distance from the sun: 1,699,530,000 miles (2,735,000,000 km).
Mean velocity in orbit: 4·23 miles (6·8 km) per second.
Tilt of axis: 98°.
Escape velocity: 13·67 miles (22 km) per second.
Force of gravity at surface: 0·93 of the earth.
Atmosphere: main constituents are hydrogen, helium, methane.
Known satellites: 15.
Discoverer: William Herschel, March 13, 1781.

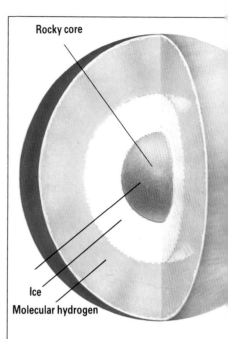

Rocky core

Ice

Molecular hydrogen

▼ Although it is much smaller than Jupiter and Saturn, Uranus is still a giant planet, made up mainly of hydrogen. It probably has a rocky core about the size of the earth. Only very faint cloudy bands can be seen on its surface. It was the first planet to be discovered with a telescope. Sir William Herschel came across it while observing from his garden, using a homemade instrument.

▲ The two known satellites of Neptune are shown in this photograph. Nereid, near the bottom right-hand corner, is only about 186 miles (300 kilometers) across. It takes almost a year to go around a very elongated orbit that swings it from 621,370 to 3,700,000 miles (one million to six million kilometers) away from Neptune.

Triton is very close to the planet, only 220,000 miles (355,000 kilometers) away, and takes less than five days to complete an orbit. It is about 2,300 miles (3,700 kilometers) across, larger than our own moon. Neptune, like its brother Uranus, may have a faint ring system waiting to be detected.

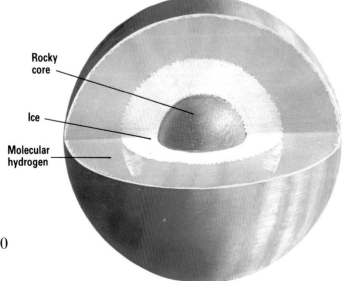

Rocky core

Ice

Molecular hydrogen

Planets

◀ Neptune was known to exist before it was discovered in 1846, because its gravitational pull was dragging Uranus from the orbit it should have been following. Although it is about four times the diameter of the earth, it is so remote that it shows only as a tiny disk, even when a very powerful telescope is used. Uranus and Neptune are very similar planets.

Few people realize that Neptune is now the farthest planet from the sun. The orbit of Pluto, which is usually known as the outermost planet, sometimes brings it closer to the sun than Neptune. This happened in 1979, and not until the year 2000 will Pluto once more mark the frontier of the solar system.

Neptune can be seen with binoculars, looking like a dim star, once its position in the sky has been plotted on a star chart.

◀ Distant Pluto was discovered in 1930, after a long and patient search. When these two photographs, taken three nights apart, were compared, the stars were all in the same place. The planet, which looked like a faint star, had moved because of its motion around the sun.

Pluto is too dim to be seen at all without a powerful telescope, and our knowledge of its surface and composition is mainly guesswork. The way its orbit is loosely linked with the orbit of Neptune suggests that it may be an escaped satellite.

Earth   Pluto

FACTS ABOUT PLUTO

Diameter: about 1,900 miles (3,000 km).
Density: about the same as that of water.
Mass: about 0·002 of the earth.
Temperature of surface: about −380°F.
Length of year: 247·7 years.
Rotation period: 6 days 9 hours.
Mean distance from the sun: 3,666,260,000 miles (5,900,000,000 km).
Mean velocity in orbit: 2·92 miles (4·7 km) per second.
Tilt of axis: 115°.
Escape velocity: about 0·3 miles (0·5 km) per second.
Atmosphere: nil.
Known satellite: 1.
Discoverer: C. W. Tombaugh, March 13, 1930.

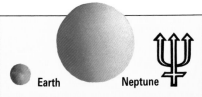

Earth   Neptune

FACTS ABOUT NEPTUNE

Diameter: about 30,000 miles (48,000 km).
Density: 1·77 times water.
Mass: 17·2 times the earth.
Temperature of cloud surface: −360°F.
Length of year: 164·8 years.
Rotation period: between 18 and 20 hours.
Mean distance from the sun: 2,794,187,000 miles (4,496,600,000 km).
Mean velocity in orbit: 3·36 miles (5·4 km) per second.
Tilt of axis: 29°.
Escape velocity: 15·5 miles (25 km) per second.
Force of gravity at surface: 1·22 times the earth.
Atmosphere: main constituents are hydrogen, helium, methane.
Known satellites: 2.
Discoverer: J. G. Galle, September 23, 1846.

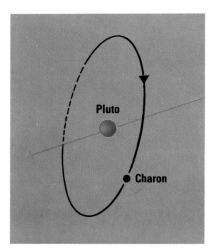

Pluto

Charon

◀ Pluto is really a double planet. Its satellite, Charon, discovered in 1978, is about 800 miles (1,300 kilometers) across. Pluto itself is only about 1,900 miles (3,000 kilometers) across. At its distance of only 12,400 miles (20,000 kilometers), Charon orbits Pluto in the same time as Pluto takes to rotate on its axis – 6 days 9 hours. This means that Charon remains stationary in Pluto's sky, and that from half of the planet it can never be seen at all. It also seems likely that Charon keeps the same hemisphere turned inward toward Pluto.

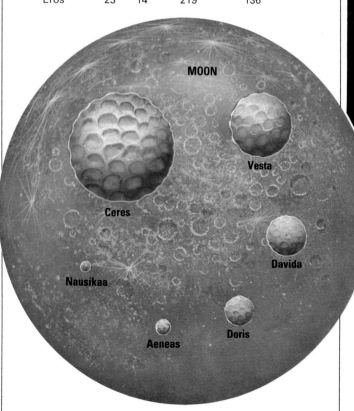

ASTEROID BELT

(Diagram labels: Adonis, Icarus, Eros, Earth, Mars, Ceres, Jupiter, Hidalgo, Saturn)

THE LARGEST ASTEROIDS

Name	Diameter (km)	(miles)	Mean distance from sun (million km)	(million miles)
Ceres	1003	623	416	258·5
Pallas	608	378	416	258·5
Vesta	538	334	354	220
Davida	323	200	478	300
Hidalgo	300	186	856	532
Aeneas	130	85	776	482
Nausikaa	94	58	360	223
Eros	23	14	219	136

(Illustration labels: MOON, Ceres, Vesta, Nausikaa, Davida, Aeneas, Doris)

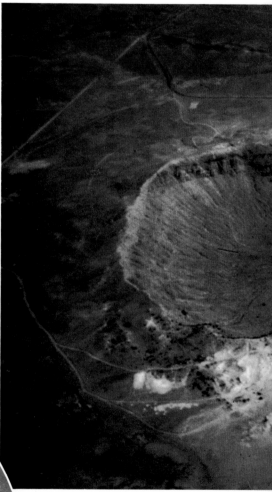

◄ The smallest major planet (Pluto) is about 1,900 miles (3,000 kilometers) across, but the solar system also contains minor planets or asteroids. The largest, Ceres, is just over 620 miles (1,000 kilometers) across, and most are less than a tenth of this size. Almost all the 2,200 known asteroids orbit in a wide belt between the orbits of Mars and Jupiter. Some, like Hidalgo, Adonis, and Icarus, have very elongated orbits that carry them near other planets. One, Chiron, lies between the orbits of Saturn and Uranus.

Astronomers believe that asteroids are the solid pieces left behind when the planets first formed. Some of these bodies plunged into the major planets, forming craters. Others crumbled into fine dust, which gives the effect of a meteor shower when it burns up at tremendous speed in the earth's atmosphere.

Debris

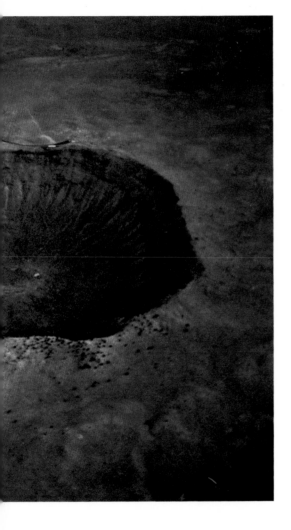

▲ The brilliant comet of 1966, called Comet Ikeya-Seki after its two discovers, could be seen easily with the naked eye. Comets are small bodies a few miles across made of crumbly rock and ice, and their elongated orbits make them swing near the sun and then far out into space. When they are near the sun, the heat releases clouds of gas and dusty particles which may stream out as a tail. Twenty or more comets may be observed each year, but most look like faint misty spots, even in a powerful telescope.

◀ The Barringer impact crater lies in the Arizona desert. It was formed between 25,000 and 50,000 years ago, when an interplanetary body about 250 feet (75 meters) across struck the surface at a speed of about 18 miles (30 kilometers) per second. This crater, which is about half a mile (just over a kilometer) across, is the best-known impact mark on the earth's surface, although there are traces of very old ones much larger than this. In its ancient past, the earth must have been scarred just like Mercury and the moon. But most of the craters have been worn away by wind and water, or flooded by lava escaping from below, as seems to have happened in some regions of Mars.

Halley's Comet

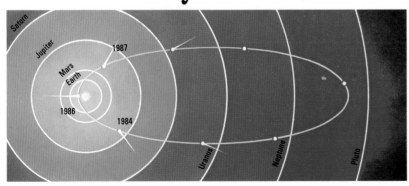

◀ Halley's Comet is famous. It returns to the sun every 76 years, and it has been observed since 240 B.C. When it appeared in 1985/6, observers in northern latitudes found it difficult to see.

Its orbital speed changes from 1·9 miles (3 kilometers) per second at its greatest distance to about 31 miles (50 kilometres) per second when nearest the sun.

The moon and planets are important to us because they are so close. But if giant Jupiter was orbiting the nearest star, it would be invisible in the largest telescope. Interstellar distances are enormous. If the sun was made into a ball 4 inches (10 centimeters) across, remote Pluto would be 1,400 feet (420 meters) away from the ball, but the nearest star would have to be placed 1,900 miles (3,000 kilometers) away.

A star is a great furnace. It starts life as a thin cloud or nebula of cold gas, much larger than the solar system. This cloud begins to collapse inward, and grows denser and hotter until it starts to glow. Eventually the atoms near the center break down and give out tremendous energy. This energy is what keeps all stars going.

Some stars are thousands of times brighter than the sun. Others are much dimmer. The very bright stars burn up quickly, and last for only a few million years, while a star like the sun will keep shining for thousands of millions of years more.

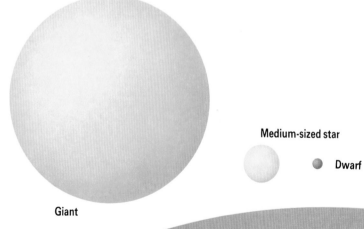

Medium-sized star

Dwarf

Giant

Supergiant

▼ Although the sun is a hundred times the diameter of the earth, some stars are more than a hundred times the diameter of the sun. Betelgeuse, the bright red star in the constellation Orion, is one of these, and is known as a supergiant. The sun is an average star.

Space

◀ The Trifid Nebula is about 2,000 light-years away from the sun (light travels 5·87 trillion miles (9·46 trillion kilometers) in one year). The distance across it is about 25,000 times the diameter of the solar system. Some of the gas is hot and shining, but huge strands of dark dust are outlined against it. The material forming the nebula is so thin that a sample the size of the earth would weigh only a few pounds. Stars are being born in nebulae like this one.

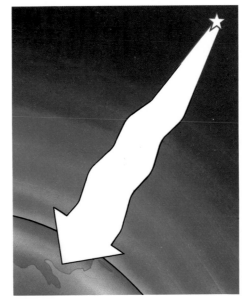

◀ On a very clear night, the stars often twinkle. This is caused by layers of warm and cool air being swirled around high in the atmosphere by strong winds. The same effect is seen over a bonfire, or over a road on a hot day. Astronomers call this effect "bad seeing," because it makes the stars look like blurred patches instead of tiny points. Not even the largest and nearest stars show a visible disk in the greatest telescopes.

▼ The Crab Nebula is the remains of a supernova, which was observed in the year 1054. The hot, fantastically dense core is at the center of this cloud of expanding wreckage.

▲ The death of a massive star, pictured here by an artist, is spectacular. As long as it keeps shining, the force of its radiation holds it in shape, like the steel girders of a building. When the radiation starts dying down, the star's material collapses in a tremendous explosion known as a supernova, which can be as bright as a whole galaxy of stars. All that is left is a tiny globe a few miles across – a neutron star. A piece of this material the size of a pinhead would weigh as much as an ocean liner.

FACTS ABOUT STARS

Stars are usually formed in groups or clusters. The sun may have been born about 4·6 billion years ago as one member of a star cluster, inside a huge nebula. The nebula has now disappeared, and all its companion stars have scattered into space. This is because stars move around in all directions at many miles per second.

Stars are being born all the time, taking the place of old stars that have burned out. Some very young ones, perhaps only a few thousand years old, can be seen attached to their nebulas. Others are still in their clusters, although the nebulas have disappeared. Then there are the countless millions of stars like the sun that have lost their clusters. Perhaps the most extraordinary groups of all are the globular clusters, gigantic balls of thousands of stars that have not broken up.

BINARY STAR SYSTEMS

Many stars are members of binary systems, which consist of two stars revolving around their barycenter. Some binary systems are so close that the stars almost touch each other, and orbit once in only a few hours. Others are much farther apart than the sun and Pluto, and one revolution takes centuries. Sometimes three or more stars may revolve around each other in a complicated way.

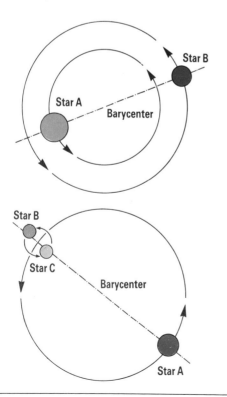

Nebulae

◄ This is the famous globular star cluster in the constellation Hercules. It is just visible with the naked eye, and contains too many stars to count (several hundred thousand) in a space about 100 light-years across. The stars in this cluster are all red giants, which are old stars that have swollen up to a colossal size, as large as the orbit of the earth or Mars. The cluster lies just outside our galaxy, so that the group has not been broken up by the gravitational pull of other stars.

About a hundred of these globular clusters are known, all scattered around the central bulge of our galaxy, and a very long way away from the sun. The distance to the Hercules cluster is about 20,000 light-years.

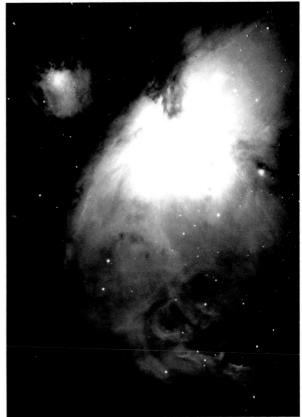

▲ The Orion Nebula is a famous naked-eye object, lying near the three "belt" stars. It is about 1,500 light-years away, and 40 light-years across. The hydrogen atoms forming the nebula shine because radiation from nearby stars makes them give out energy in the form of light – rather like an aurora in the earth's atmosphere. The dark clouds are other nebulas, nearer to the sun, which block out the light. Astronomers have observed some stars in the nebula that may have begun shining only a few years ago.

◄ The Pleiades or Seven Sisters are the most famous cluster in the sky. They lie in the constellation Taurus, and six or seven stars can be seen with the naked eye. Altogether there are several hundred stars in the cluster, but the fainter ones cannot be seen without a telescope. The bright stars are blue giants, hundreds of times brighter than the sun and much hotter. A few wisps of the old nebula from which they formed can be seen shining by light reflected from the bright stars.

The Pleiades were formed only a few million years ago, so they are some of the youngest naked-eye stars in the sky. The brightest stars, however, will only last a few million years more before they start exhausting their hydrogen supply. The much fainter stars in the cluster are more like the sun, and will shine for thousands of millions of years after the cluster breaks up.

▼ The Milky Way is the "inside" view of our own galaxy. Only someone far away in space could see what it really looks like, although astronomers have discovered ways of getting a fairly good picture. This view of the sky looking toward the center of the galaxy, in the constellation Sagittarius, shows clouds of stars and dark nebulas. The single scattered stars in the photograph are all much closer to the sun, and just happen to lie in the same direction. The streak was caused by a passing artificial satellite.

FACTS ABOUT THE MILKY WAY

Diameter: 85,000 light-years.
Thickness at center: 13,000 light-years.
Thickness through the arms: about 5,000 light-years.
Mass: 1·1 trillion times the sun.
Total brightness: 10 billion times the sun.
Total number of stars: about 100 billion.
Largest known star: IRS5 in Perseus (diameter 9,320 million miles (15,000 million km).
Nearest star to the sun: Proxima Centauri, 4·3 light-years away.
Age of galaxy: about 12 billion years.

► The Milky Way is a spiral galaxy with long, curving arms, and this is how it might look from space. The sun's position is shown by the red arrow. It lies on one of the arms, about 30,000 light-years from the center or nucleus. The stars which are crowded into the flat arms give the Milky Way the appearance of a faint band circling the sky.

Galaxies

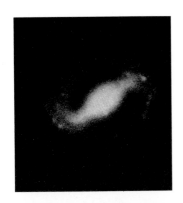

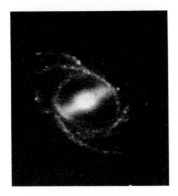

▲ Galaxies fall into several groups. Elliptical (E), have no spiral arms. Spiral (S), have arms like our galaxy, the Milky Way. Irregular galaxies (Ir), are formless. The galaxies shown here are different kinds of barred spiral (SB), where the arms come from a bar across the galaxy's center.

▲ This photograph of the famous Andromeda galaxy probably shows how our own galaxy would appear if we could see it from out in space. It is about the same size as the Milky Way, and lies about 2 million light-years from us. This means that the light reaching the earth now left the galaxy before plants and animals had appeared on our planet. The bluish color of the arms shows that they contain young stars and plenty of dust. The yellowish nucleus contains red giants, which are old stars. The two small patches are satellite galaxies. The Andromeda galaxy can be seen with the naked eye on a clear night, and binoculars show the satellite galaxies as well.

FACTS ABOUT GALAXIES

A galaxy like ours contains about 100 billion stars, but there are more galaxies than this number in the universe. More powerful telescopes keep revealing fainter and fainter galaxies, farther and farther away. The most distant so far detected are over 10 billion light-years away. The farther away a galaxy is, the faster it is traveling away from us. The most distant are moving almost at the speed of light.

Astronomers have worked out that all the galaxies must have been close together about 20 billion years ago. If this is right, then all the material in the universe must have started flying apart in the Big Bang at that time.

As well as galaxies, there are quasars. These appear to be much smaller than ordinary galaxies, but send out hundreds of times as much energy. Quasars are all so far away that we cannot see them in detail. They may be the very bright and hot centers of distant galaxies.

The original telescope was the human eye. In dim conditions, its opening or aperture is about 0·3 inches (8 millimeters). With this "telescope" we can see thousands of stars. But a proper astronomical telescope has a lens or mirror much larger than the eye, so that it collects much more light and makes stars and other night-sky objects look far brighter. It also brings many fainter stars into view. A telescope with an aperture of about 4 inches (100 millimeters) can show a million stars in the sky. Telescopes also magnify, so that things look larger.

Most astronomical telescopes use a mirror, and they are known as reflectors. Telescopes which use a lens are called refractors. There are also radio telescopes, which pick up radiation that cannot be seen or photographed.

THE HISTORY OF THE TELESCOPE

1608: The first refracting telescope is invented in Holland by Jan Lippershey.
1609: Galileo makes his first astronomical observations with a telescope.
1668: Isaac Newton makes the first reflecting telescope.
1789: William Herschel builds his huge 48-inch (1·2-meter) reflector.
1897: The largest-ever refractor, aperture 40 inches (1 meter) completed, Yerkes Observatory, Wisconsin.
1948: The 200-inch (5·1-meter) reflector is installed at Mount Palomar, U.S.A.
1976: The 20-foot (6-meter) reflector is completed at Zelenchukskaya, Caucasus, USSR.
1986?: Launch of the 8-foot (2·4-meter) Space Telescope.

LARGEST RADIO TELESCOPES

Aperture	
1,000 ft (305 m)	Arecibo, Puerto Rico, 1963
330 ft (100 m)	Effelsberg, West Germany, 1976
300 ft (91 m)	Green Bank, West Virginia, U.S.A., 1962
250 ft (76 m)	Jodrell Bank, England, 1957

◀ The largest steerable radio telescope in the world is this 328-foot (100-meter) aperture dish at Effelsberg in West Germany. It can point anywhere in the sky, unlike the enormous 1,000-foot (305-meter) bowl at Arecibo, which can only observe objects overhead. A telescope like this can detect objects that cannot be seen at all, such as the very center of our galaxy, which is hidden by dark nebulas. Radio waves from the nucleus can pass through the dust, but visible light cannot. The galaxy has been mapped by radio waves.

Space

◄ A large observatory, Mount Stromlo, near Canberra in Australia. A modern observatory is the size of a village, and Mount Stromlo is one of the largest in the southern hemisphere. Its biggest telescope is a 6-foot (1·9-meter) reflector, but it contains four other large instruments, each one housed in a separate dome. The domes are painted silver to reflect away the sun's heat. This is so that the air inside does not warm up during the day and make the telescopic images unsteady when work begins at night. The hill on which the observatory is built is 2,500 feet (768 meters) high. Almost all observatories are built high up, above the worst of the dirt and fog, to give the best possible view of the sky.

KITT PEAK OBSERVATORY

◄ This unique telescope is at the Kitt Peak Observatory, Arizona, for observing the sun. The flat, movable mirror turns slowly during the day to follow the sun as it moves across the sky. The light from this mirror is focused by the concave mirror. It forms an image of the sun about 31 inches (80 centimeters) across below ground level, in the observing room, where sunspots and other details on the sun's surface can be examined in great detail. The long spectrograph can be used to analyze the light and find out what elements are in the sun, and the temperature and make-up of its surface.

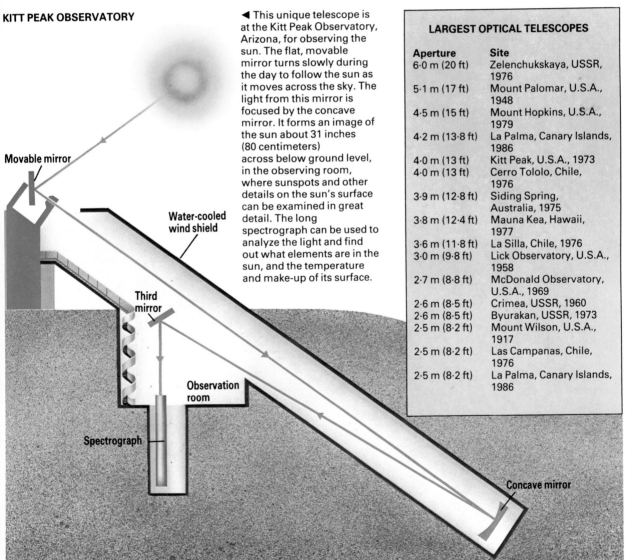

Movable mirror

Water-cooled wind shield

Third mirror

Observation room

Spectrograph

Concave mirror

LARGEST OPTICAL TELESCOPES	
Aperture	**Site**
6·0 m (20 ft)	Zelenchukskaya, USSR, 1976
5·1 m (17 ft)	Mount Palomar, U.S.A., 1948
4·5 m (15 ft)	Mount Hopkins, U.S.A., 1979
4·2 m (13·8 ft)	La Palma, Canary Islands, 1986
4·0 m (13 ft)	Kitt Peak, U.S.A., 1973
4·0 m (13 ft)	Cerro Tololo, Chile, 1976
3·9 m (12·8 ft)	Siding Spring, Australia, 1975
3·8 m (12·4 ft)	Mauna Kea, Hawaii, 1977
3·6 m (11·8 ft)	La Silla, Chile, 1976
3·0 m (9·8 ft)	Lick Observatory, U.S.A., 1958
2·7 m (8·8 ft)	McDonald Observatory, U.S.A., 1969
2·6 m (8·5 ft)	Crimea, USSR, 1960
2·6 m (8·5 ft)	Byurakan, USSR, 1973
2·5 m (8·2 ft)	Mount Wilson, U.S.A., 1917
2·5 m (8·2 ft)	Las Campanas, Chile, 1976
2·5 m (8·2 ft)	La Palma, Canary Islands, 1986

Rockets

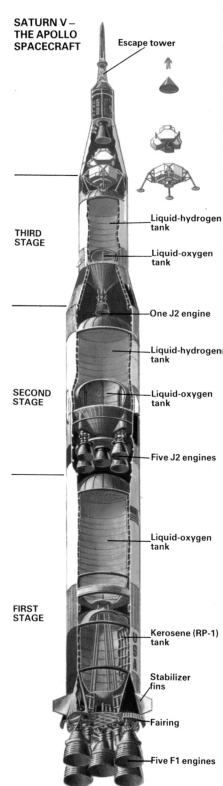

SATURN V – THE APOLLO SPACECRAFT

- Escape tower
- Liquid-hydrogen tank
- Liquid-oxygen tank
- One J2 engine
- Liquid-hydrogen tank
- Liquid-oxygen tank
- Five J2 engines
- Liquid-oxygen tank
- Kerosene (RP-1) tank
- Stabilizer fins
- Fairing
- Five F1 engines

THIRD STAGE

SECOND STAGE

FIRST STAGE

▲ Apollo 11 takes off for the moon in 1969. In only eleven years, the United States had made the amazing jump from launching its first earth satellite, Explorer 1, weighing only 26 pounds (12 kilograms), on January 31, 1958, to sending three men into orbit around the moon and landing two of them safely on the surface. One reason was that rocket boosters became much more dependable and powerful. Also, the silicon chip made computers much smaller and lighter, leaving more room in the spacecraft for men and instruments. Finally, billions of dollars were spent on the project.

▶ This cutaway drawing shows a complete Apollo rocket, ready for launch. Like most space probes, most of what stands on the launch pad never escapes from the earth's atmosphere at all. The weight of the whole spacecraft was about 2,900 tons, but only about 30,865 pounds (14,000 kilograms) of this reached the moon.

Like Apollo, most deep-space rockets have three main stages. The first stage raises the craft as high as possible, 41 miles (66 kilometers) in the case of Apollo. It then separates and falls back to the ground. The second stage, which is smaller, takes over, rises to a much greater height, but also falls back. The third stage gives the final kick to break the payload free of the earth's gravity.

Satellites

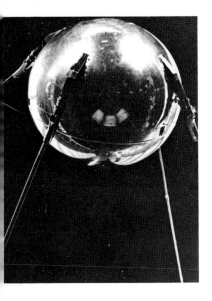

SOME SPACE FIRSTS

1957: Sputnik 1 launched – the first earth satellite.
1959: Luna 2 hits the moon.
1961: The first man in space, Yuri Gagarin, orbits the earth once in Vostok 1.
1962: Mariner 2 passes near Venus.
1967: Venera 3 makes a successful landing on Venus.
1969–1972: Six successful Apollo manned lunar landings.
1973: Pioneer 10 takes close-up photographs of Jupiter.
1974: Mariner 10 takes close-up photographs of Mercury.
1976: First successful landings on Mars, by two Viking spacecraft.
1979: Pioneer 11 takes close-up photographs of Saturn.
1981: First launch of the Space Shuttle.

Vostok 1

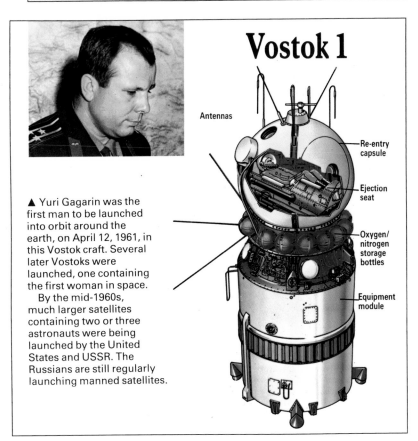

Antennas

Re-entry capsule

Ejection seat

Oxygen/ nitrogen storage bottles

Equipment module

▲ Sputnik 1 was launched from the Soviet space center at Tyuratam, in Central Asia, on October 4, 1957. It was the first man-made satellite, and could orbit the earth in 96 minutes. It came as a complete surprise. Nobody in the United States or Europe had realized that the Russians would be able to launch a satellite. It signaled the start of the "space race." The Russians were the first to hit the moon with a space probe, and the first to launch a man into orbit. The first men on the moon, however, were American.

▲ Yuri Gagarin was the first man to be launched into orbit around the earth, on April 12, 1961, in this Vostok craft. Several later Vostoks were launched, one containing the first woman in space.

By the mid-1960s, much larger satellites containing two or three astronauts were being launched by the United States and USSR. The Russians are still regularly launching manned satellites.

An Eye on the Weather

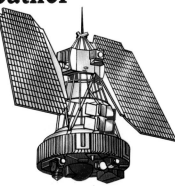

◄ Satellites can be used for many purposes besides carrying astronauts. Some have been used for relaying messages and television programs to different places on the earth's surface. Others, such as this Nimbus satellite, record the cloud patterns in the atmosphere to help forecasting. The large panels collect solar energy for powering the instruments.

LUNAR EXCURSION MODULE

Radio antennas

Docking hatch

Docking target

Rendezvous radar antenna

Ascent Stage

Window

Control thrusters

Fuel tank

Hatch

Egress platform

Descent Stage

Descent engine nozzle

Landing gear

Race to

◄ The Apollo lander, or lunar excursion module (LEM). This fragile craft was stored safely inside a protective shield until the third stage of the rocket and the moonship were in earth orbit. It was then carried into lunar orbit attached to the front of the command module, which released it so that the two-man crew could descend to the lunar surface. Only the upper part, the ascent stage, took off from the surface to rejoin the command module in orbit. Once the astronauts had crawled through the docking hatch into the command module, the ascent stage was sent down to crash onto the moon.

The LEM stood 23 feet (7 meters) high, and on the earth's surface, complete with astronauts, weighed 33,000 pounds (15,000 kilograms), 24,000 pounds (11,000 kilograms) of this being fuel for the engines. On the moon, however, it weighed only one-sixth as much, because of the very low gravity. Every spare ounce of weight was cut away; the outer metallic skin was not much thicker than tissue paper.

THE STORY OF APOLLO

The Apollo program began on May 25, 1961, when President Kennedy announced that men would be sent to the moon by the end of the decade. A disaster occurred in 1967 when three astronauts died in the lunar craft while training on the ground. The first practice flight was in 1968 in Apollo 7, and Apollo 8 took its crew of three astronauts around the moon, without landing, at Christmas that year. The first landing was made in 1969. The following six Apollo flights went according to plan except for Apollo 13, which had vital equipment destroyed in an explosion during the outward journey, and had to return to earth without landing.

THE APOLLO LANDINGS

Apollo 11: July 16–24, 1969; Mare Tranquillitatis.
Apollo 12: November 14–24, 1969; Oceanus Procellarum.
Apollo 13: April 11–17, 1970; no landing.
Apollo 14: January 31–February 9, 1971; Oceanus Procellarum.
Apollo 15: July 26–August 7, 1971; Apennine Mountains.
Apollo 16: April 16–27, 1972; Descartes crater in the lunar highlands.
Apollo 17: December 7–19, 1972; Mare Serenitatis.

▼ A photograph taken from the Apollo 11 command module when it was in orbit around the moon. The distant earth shines in the black sky, and the separated lunar module is only a few yards away.

the Moon

These are two of the Soviet probes that have been sent to the moon. Luna 3 went round the moon in 1959 and sent back the first photograph showing its far side. Lunar 13 made a soft landing on the moon in December 1966, and sent excellent photographs of the surface back to earth. An earlier probe, Luna 9, made the first controlled landing in February 1966. The later Luna probes, starting with number 16 in September 1970, have dug soil from the surface and sent it back to earth using an automatic spacecraft.

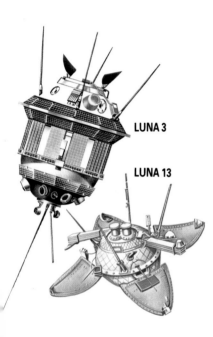

LUNA 3

LUNA 13

Mission Control in Houston, Texas, was the nerve center for all space flights once the rocket had left the ground. Radio signals from the spacecraft were received by special tracking stations situated around the world, and relayed to this operations room.

▲ Edwin Aldrin, the second man on the moon, photographed by the first man, Neil Armstrong. Already, the lunar soil is showing many footprints, which will remain unchanged for millions of years. The helmet visor has been coated to protect the astronaut's face from dangerous radiation. Since the moon's sky is black, shadows are very dark, and the astronauts found it difficult to see things shaded from direct sunlight. The large pack on Aldrin's back is the portable life support system (PLSS), which contained enough oxygen to last four hours, with an extra 30 minutes emergency supply. It also contained a radio for speaking to Armstrong, the command module in orbit, and direct to Mission Control at Houston.

Skylab

THE SKYLAB CREWS

First crew: Conrad, Kerwin, Weitz;
May 25 to June 22 (28 days).
Second crew: Bean, Garriott, Lousma;
July 28 to September 25 (59 days).
Third crew: Carr, Pogue, Gibson;
November 16 to February 8 (84 days).

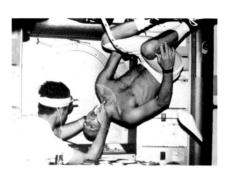

▲ In the weightless conditions of space, one of the members of the first Skylab crew carries out a dental check without needing a reclining chair.

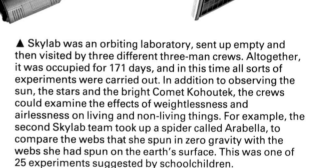

▲ Skylab was an orbiting laboratory, sent up empty and then visited by three different three-man crews. Altogether, it was occupied for 171 days, and in this time all sorts of experiments were carried out. In addition to observing the sun, the stars and the bright Comet Kohoutek, the crews could examine the effects of weightlessness and airlessness on living and non-living things. For example, the second Skylab team took up a spider called Arabella, to compare the webs that she spun in zero gravity with the webs she had spun on the earth's surface. This was one of 25 experiments suggested by schoolchildren.

Skylab also had some anxious moments. One of the sun shields was damaged, and the first crew had to repair it before they could go inside. Some of the astronauts found that weightlessness made them feel sick. But on the whole, Skylab was a triumphant success.

▼ History was made in July 1975, when two spacecraft launched from the U.S.A. and the USSR locked together, 140 miles (225 kilometers) above the earth's surface. This drawing shows the two craft approaching each other, with a special docking collar attached to the Apollo capsule. This capsule is the same as the command module used in the trips to the moon. The Soviet craft is a Soyuz satellite. Many of these two-man satellites have been launched. The two craft in this unique Apollo–Soyuz experiment remained locked together for two days before separating and returning to earth.

SPACE PROBES

Mariner 9 (U.S.A.): Mars, 1971 (orbiter).
Venera 8 (USSR): Venus, 1972 (landed).
Pioneer 10 (U.S.A.): Jupiter, 1973 (flyby).
Pioneer 11 (U.S.A.): Jupiter, 1974 (flyby); Saturn, 1979 (flyby).
Mariner 10 (U.S.A.): Venus and Mercury, 1974 (flyby).
Venera 9 & 10 (USSR): Venus, 1975 (landed).
Viking 1 & 2 (U.S.A.): Mars, 1976 (landed).
Venera 11 & 12 (USSR): Venus, 1978 (landed).
Pioneer 12 (U.S.A.): Venus, 1978 (orbiter).
Voyager 1 (U.S.A.): Jupiter, 1979 and Saturn, 1980 (flyby).
Voyager 2 (U.S.A.): Jupiter, 1979 and Saturn, 1981 (flyby).
Vega 1 & 2 (USSR): Venus, 1985 (flyby).

▼ The two Voyager spacecraft, launched in 1977, are now heading towards the outer planets. Their first target was Jupiter, which Voyager 1 passed on March 5, 1979 and Voyager 2 passed on July 9. They took close-up photographs of Jupiter's five inner satellites as well as of the planet itself. The gravitational pull of Jupiter made them swing into a new path toward Saturn, which Voyager 1 passed on November 12, 1980, photographing surface, rings, and satellites in great detail. The pull of Saturn has now turned it into a new path, and it is heading toward outer space, never to return. Voyager 2, which passed Saturn in August 1981, had a rendezvous with the outer planet Uranus in January 1986. Neptune may be observed from close range in 1989. The sizes of the planets are not shown to scale.

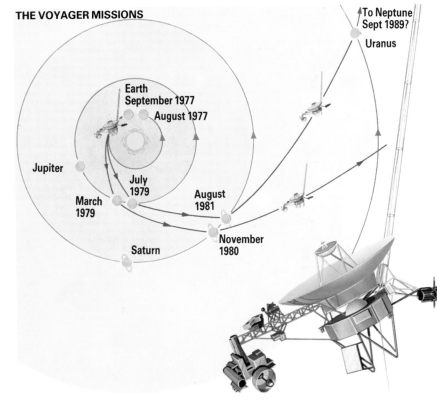

THE VOYAGER MISSIONS

To Neptune Sept 1989?
Uranus
Earth September 1977
August 1977
Jupiter
July 1979
March 1979
August 1981
November 1980
Saturn

▲ One of the most successful planetary probes, Mariner 10, took this photograph of Mercury's craters in 1974.

PROBES TO MARS

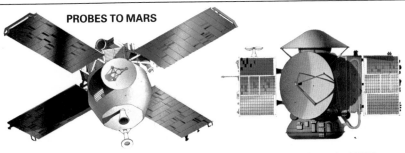

▲ Mariner 9 went into orbit around Mars in 1971, and sent back the first good close-up photographs of another planet.

▲ Mars 3, launched from the USSR, was the first probe to make a soft landing on Mars, in 1971 but it did not send back any information.

▲ The two Viking landers which reached Mars in 1976 sent back information about the surface conditions, photographed the landscape, and searched for signs of life.

◄ The Space Shuttle blasts off on the back of its huge fuel tank, powered by the two long booster rockets on either side as well as by the main engines. The Shuttle is a reusable spacecraft.

SHUTTLE MISSION HIGHLIGHTS

1981: First flight of Shuttle Columbia.
1982: Fifth flight. First commercial payload – two communications satellites.
1983: Sixth flight. Maiden flight of Shuttle Challenger.
1983: Seventh flight. Sally Ride first American woman in space.
1983: Ninth flight. European Spacelab 1 carried into orbit.
1984: Tenth flight. Astronauts perform the first-ever spacewalk untethered to a spacecraft.
1984: Eleventh flight. Capture and repair of a satellite launched in 1980.
1986: Twenty-fifth flight. Seven astronauts killed when Shuttle Challenger explodes.

▼ The Shuttle is launched (**1**) with its own engine and the two booster rockets firing. At a height of about 27 miles (43 kilometers), the boosters are empty and parachuted back into the ocean for recovery (**2**). Once the Shuttle has reached orbit under its own power, the large empty fuel tank is detached (**3**). The cargo (which may be an experimental package, or replacement astronauts) is unloaded (**4**). To return to the earth, the Shuttle plunges nose-downward into the atmosphere and glides back to the ground (**5**). Only the empty fuel tank is wasted.

2

3

4

1

5

Shuttle

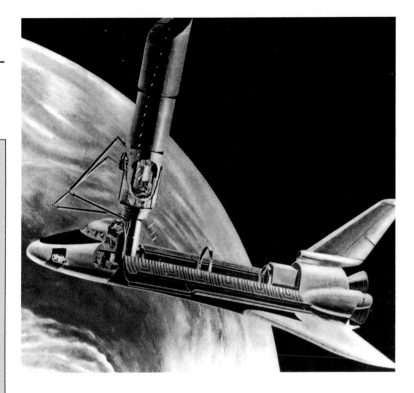

FACTS ABOUT SPACE SHUTTLE

ngth: 122 ft (37·2 m).

ngspan: 78 ft (23·8 m).

rgo bay: length 60 ft (18·3 m), diameter
ft (4·6 m).

tal ground weight: 170,000 lbs
,000 kg).

rgo weight: 65,035 lbs (29,500 kg)
ximum.

el tank: length 154 ft (46·9 m), diameter
ft (8·2 m).

mber of crew: 4.

ximum number of passengers: 6.

rmal orbit height: 50–93 miles
–150 km).

ximum orbit height: 621 miles
00 km).

ne spent in orbit: 7–30 days.

st of each flight: about $10,000,000.

st launch: April 12, 1981.

bable number of launches per year: 10 to

mber of shuttles operating: 3.

unch sites: Florida (low orbit), California
gh orbit).

ncipal landing sites: California and
rida.

ergency landing sites: 15, scattered
und the world.

▲ An impression of how the 7·8-foot (2·4-meter) aperture Space Telescope may look when it is carried into an orbit about 370 miles (600 kilometers) above the earth's surface in 1986. With two solar panels to charge its batteries, it will be controlled from the earth's surface. Free from the dirt and unsteadiness of our atmosphere, it will be able to record distant galaxies in much greater detail than is possible now, and might even detect planets around nearby stars.

Columbia, the first Space Shuttle, nds at Edwards Air Force Base in California after the first Space ransportation System Flight (STS-) in April 1981. Now in regular peration, the shuttle can carry cientific experimental packages nto orbit. It has also been used to epair and rescue satellites, and everal Spacelabs (container-type aboratories) have been carried aloft nd brought back to earth. Some ommunications companies have aid to have their satellites taken up the shuttle and left in orbit; it is ven possible that future flights may nclude fare-paying passengers.

Index

Acknowledgements

Photographs: page 1 Nasa; 3 California Institute of Technology; 6/7 Robin Kerrod *center*, P. Moore *bottom*; 7 Lockheed Solar Laboratory *top and bottom*; 9 & 10 Nasa; 13 Satour *top*, Nasa *bottom*; 14 Nasa *center and bottom*; 16–19 Nasa; 20 & 21 Royal Astronomical Society; 22 US Travel Service *center*; 23 US Naval Observatory; 24 & 25 California Institute of Technology; 26 US Naval Observatory *top*; 27 California Institute of Technology *top and bottom*; 28 US Naval Observatory; 29 California Institute of Technology; 30 Max Plank Institute for Radio Astronomy; 31 Australia News and Information Bureau; 32 Nasa; 33 Nasa *top and bottom*, Novosti Press Agency *center*; 34–39 Nasa.